KEEPER OF THE LIGHT
by STCS R. E. Matuska

The smog, an ominous
foreboding shroud engulfs the rock and light,
and many a ship might run aground
on this dark and moonless night.
But the beacon cuts through the smog
and mist
for the Wickie makes it shine,
and a sailor knows without his light
the shore's impossible to find.
The man in the light is older than the sea
his beard as white as meershaum,
but soon the old man will be replaced
and his light will shine alone.
For in his place an electronic wizard
as cold as a Nor' Easter gale,
will guide the light without a heart
and all ships under sail.
For eons the man has watched the sea
in all it's fury and rage,
but who remembers his vigilance now
in this "modern" day and age.
The sailor's wives, mothers, and children
are the ones who will remember,
their shipwrecked sailors the old man saved
on that night in late November.
For the old man didn't drag his anchor
as he went for the boat and crew,
on a nigh blacker than a peacoat's button
in a fog thicker than stew.
In a pounding surf he manned the helm
heading for the schooner's crew,
and after guiding the surfboat ashore
gave 'em shelter, warmth, and brew.
No more will sailors on windswept decks
look upon the beacon's light,
and feel the warmth and friendship there
on cold and lonely nights.
The long nights are much more colder now
the wind is chilling to the bone,
the beacon's light less bright somehow
the heart feels more alone.
But His light can never be replaced
if only we share it together,
then like the eternal flame that burns
its glow will last forever.
For the light that shines from Him is in us
a light that has stood the test
and we are the keepers of His light
the warmest and the best.

The most complete pictorial guide presently available of the historic lighthouses of Massachusetts.

Foreword

Early in the history of this country Massachusetts became a center of commerce and shipping. This made lighthouses especially important on its islands and shores.

Loss of life and cargo due to shipwrecks demanded an effective system of lighthouses. The first American lighthouse was built in Boston Harbor on Little Brewster Island. This light and the more than sixty others which were added have served well to guide safely home those who "went down to the sea in ships."

Many lighthouses have been discontinued as navigational aids and are now privately owned. Most of the private owners recognize that as custodians of historic treasures they have an obligation to preserve and to some extent share these former government properties.

Some private owners seek more privacy and make it necessary for devotees of these lighthouses to see and photograph them from the air, water, or if on land from behind "No Trespassing" signs. We respect the wishes of those who desire privacy. It is a matter of public record but we have not included the names of these owners in this book.

Fortunately, most private owners have done an excellent job of preserving and maintaining these historic edifices which if left to the elements or vandals would have been destroyed. The U.S. Coast Guard is also now doing a better job of safeguarding the future of the lighthouses which they discontinue.

Most discontinued lights are now being placed in the hands of non-profit preservation groups or community governments to be maintained and protected. Several have museums connected with them which endeavor to share the lore and memorabilia of the sites with the public.

We have visited the sites of each of these lights personally in order to photograph them. This has been a distinct pleasure and we would recommend it to you. We have had many letters from excited lighthouse enthusiasts who have used our books on Maine and Rhode Island lighthouses as a guide for their visits. We hope you will get as much enjoyment from this book.

We have listed the lighthouses of Massachusetts generally in geographic order as they are located from South to North. A map is included to help you locate them.

The Historical Commission of the Commonwealth of Massachusetts is to be commended for its efforts to include most of the lighthouses of the state in the National Register of Historic Places. Forty-two Massachusetts lighthouses are currently listed in the "Register". We are indebted to the Commission for information we have gleaned from their research.

We urge you to be active in the movement to preserve America's lighthouses. There are several organizations you can join in this cause. We will list those we know of and also some of the lighthouse museums you could visit. A bibliography for further reading will also be included.

Best wishes to you as you explore the lighthouses of Massachusetts!

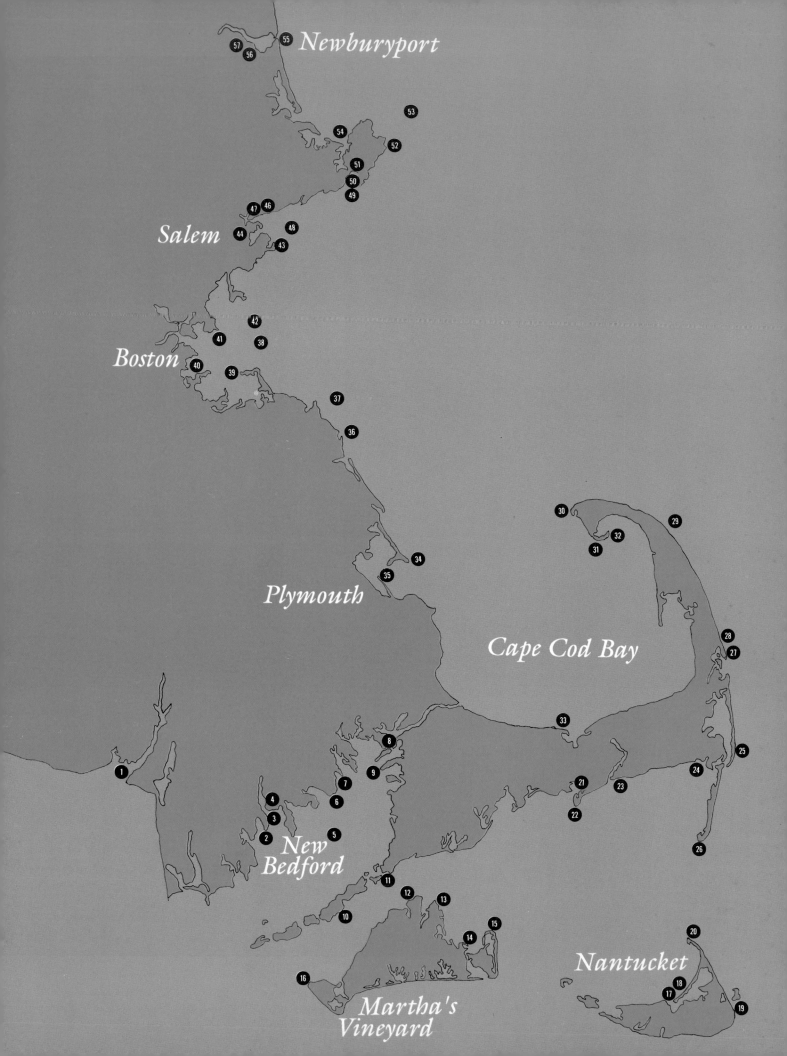

Newburyport

Salem

Boston

Plymouth

Cape Cod Bay

New
Bedford

Martha's
Vineyard

Nantucket

Lighthouses of Massachusetts

Lightships

New Bedford
Nantucket

Nantucket I
Nantucket II

Lighthouses of New Hampshire

Isles of Shoals
Fort Point
Whaleback

BORDEN FLATS LIGHTHOUSE

(White light flashing every 2.5 seconds)

This lighthouse is just south of the Braga Bridge in Taunton River in the town of Fall River. It was built in 1881 and is now an unmanned light operated by the Coast Guard. This caisson type light warns shipping of shallow water and the reef upon which it is built. It consists of a basement, first floor, lantern room and lens room. A large porch surrounds the first floor.

The name "Borden Flats" derives from a prominent Fall River family who owned extensive textile mills along the river in the area.

BUTLER FLATS LIGHTHOUSE

(White light flashing every 4 seconds)

This light built in 1898 is located in the New Bedford Channel of the New Bedford Harbor (Acushnet River). As a manned light this station was staffed by five enlisted men and two officers who maintained the light and fog signal.

The Coast Guard decided in 1975 that the light was no longer needed after a light and fog signal was placed on the Hurricane Barrier closer to the harbor.

Operation of the light as a private aid was begun by the city of New Bedford in 1979 under license from the Department of Transportation. A private group known as The Coast Guard Commemorative Exhibit is concerned with the preservation and maintenance of this lighthouse.

This lighthouse is unique in that the tower above the cast iron caisson is constructed primarily of brick.

CLARK'S POINT LIGHTHOUSE

Historical records indicate that land was donated to the government for the construction of a lighthouse on Clark's Point in the year 1800. It was relocated to the top of Fort Taber in 1869. This area now known as the Fort Rodman Military Reservation was the site of activity from the time of the Revolutionary War to the time of World War II.

This now abandoned and inactive lighthouse is in a state of disrepair. The city of New Bedford, however, is now in the process of acquiring Fort Taber from the Federal Government and plans to rehabilitate the area for use as a military museum and park.

PALMER ISLAND LIGHTHOUSE

This light, now inactive and abandoned, was built in 1849 and served until 1941 when its light was automated and transferred to Butler Flats Lighthouse.

The light served for nearly 100 years in bustling New Bedford Harbor which for many years was the home of one of the world's largest whaling and fishing fleets.

Several major storms threatened the light. A hurricane in 1938 destroyed the keeper's house. The keeper, Captain Arthur A. Small, was injured and his wife was drowned as they attempted to reach the light.

This lighthouse has suffered much damage by fire and vandalism since being deactivated. Prominent in the history of New Bedford (it is pictured as a part of the official city seal) there is interest in it being restored and made part of a proposed park on Palmer Island.

NED POINT LIGHTHOUSE
(White light flashing for 6 seconds each 6 seconds)

This still active light was built in 1837 on four acres of land purchased by the Government from H.H. Edwards for $240. It was purchased through his guardian Barnabus Hiller.

The station originally included a keeper's dwelling and barn, an oil house, and lighthouse tower. Only the latter two remain. The keeper's dwelling was moved by barge across Buzzard's Bay to the Wing's Neck Light Station in Pocasset in 1930. The 35 foot light tower is built of white washed stone. The town of Mattapoisett now operates a park in the area around the light tower. The Coast Guard retains only .17 of an acre for the tower and a right of way through the park.

BUZZARD'S BAY LIGHT
(White light flashing every 2.5 seconds)

This Texas tower type light built in 1961 marks the entrance to Buzzard's Bay. It is an active light maintained and operated by the U.S. Coast Guard. A helicopter landing pad on top of the structure facilitates servicing this navigational aid.

BIRD ISLAND LIGHTHOUSE
(White light flashing each 6 seconds)

This lighthouse built in 1819 on Bird Island is just south of Butler Point on the east side of Sippican Harbor, opposite the town of Marion. The tower built of masonry is now a private navigational aid maintained by the Sippican Historical Society. It was sold to the town of Marion in 1939 after a hurricane destroyed the dwelling attached and the other outbuildings in 1938. The high water mark during the hurricane was sixteen feet up from the foundation of the twenty-five foot tower.

The property which is an island at high water was sold to the U.S. Government by George and Betty Blankenship in 1819 for $200.

CLEVELAND LEDGE LIGHTHOUSE
(White light flashing each 10 seconds)

This lighthouse was built in 1941 but not lit until 1943 due to the war. It is the most recent lighthouse station established in Massachusetts. Two miles from shore between Hog Neck Peninsula and Mashnee Island the light is built on a ledge in 21 feet of water. It serves to aid shipping entering and leaving the west end of the Cape Cod Canal.

The light station consists of a two story dwelling on a 52 foot wide caisson foundation. The lighthouse tower sits atop the dwelling and reaches 74 feet above the water.

During a 1944 hurricane, only the valiant efforts of the crew kept the station operating when tons of water poured in through an opening created by a block which was dislodged by the battering of the waves. The light was automated in 1978 and the Coast Guard keepers were removed.

WING'S NECK LIGHTHOUSE

Built in 1849, this lighthouse station located at the end of the Wing's Neck Peninsula and near the Buzzard's Bay end of the Cape Cod Canal, figures prominently in the records of lifesaving endeavors by light keepers. This light replaced by a steel skeleton tower in 1945 is no longer an active light.

It was sold to become a private dwelling in 1947. The lighthouse compound marked by "No Trespassing" signs is most easily seen from the air or by boat.

The former lighthouse station includes the original 1849 oil house and a second keeper's house which was moved from Ned Point light station in 1870. A fire destroyed a portion of the lighthouse in 1878 and in 1889 a new keeper's dwelling and tower were constructed.

National attention was attracted to this lighthouse station in 1932 when the keepers, brothers George and William Howard, saved eight lives between January 1 and August 30.

During his career as a keeper William Howard was credited with saving at least 37 lives. We wonder who will provide these services of heroism now that most of the lights are automated and unmanned.

Perhaps ship to shore radios, Coast Guard cutters, and helicopters are filling some of this need for mariners in distress.

TARPAULIN COVE
LIGHTHOUSE
(White light flashing every 6 seconds)

Originally established in 1817, this lighthouse station is located on the west side of Tarpaulin Cove which is on the southwesterly shore of Naushon Island.

Naushon is the largest of the Elizabeth Islands and lies between Buzzard's Bay and Vineyard Sound.

The tower now standing was built in 1856. The keeper's dwelling and other outbuildings were demolished in 1962 after they had become badly deteriorated.

A marker on the site states that "This cove was widely used in sailing days as a shelter during storms or while awaiting favorable winds.

Pirates used it in the 17th century as a base to prey on shipping in the Sound ... a small village was located here in early days."

NOBSKA POINT LIGHTHOUSE

(White light with red sector flashing each 6 seconds)

Located at Nobska Point overlooking Wood's Hole Harbor and just south of Falmouth, this light station established in 1828 is a major navigational aid between Buzzard's Bay and Vineyard Sound.

The tower originally built on top of the keeper's dwelling was replaced in 1876 with an iron tower lined with brick. Another keeper's dwelling was also built at this time. A second keeper's house was added in 1900.

Unmanned and automated in 1985, the station now provides a dwelling for the Wood's Hole group commander.

WEST CHOP
LIGHTHOUSE
*(White light occulting each 4 seconds with
3 seconds light)*

A lighthouse tower and keeper's
dwelling were built of stone in 1817.
Due to encroachment of the ocean a
new tower and dwelling were built in
1891. This 52 foot tower built of
brick is the one in use at this time.

The lighthouse is located in Tisbury,
Martha's Vineyard, on the west side
of the entrance to Vineyard Haven
Harbor. Although an active light it
is unmanned and automated.

EAST CHOP
LIGHTHOUSE
(Equal interval green light each 6 seconds)

This site was established in 1828 as
part of a semiphore system which
extended from Edgartown across
Cape Cod, the south shore of
Massachusetts, and to the Central
Wharf in Boston Harbor. It served
to notify ships owners of sightings
off Martha's Vineyard. Also known
as Telegraph Hill, the site is located
on the highest bluff of East Chop,
Martha's Vineyard.

A wooden structure was built by
Captain Silas Daggett in 1869 with
contributions of local Martha's
Vineyard merchants. The tower
burned down the same year and was
rebuilt in 1872. The U.S.
Government purchased the site for
$5000 in 1875 and within a year
established a lighthouse station with
a cast iron tower, keeper's dwelling,
and outbuildings. Only the tower
remains at this time. It is automated
and unmanned.

EDGARTOWN HARBOR LIGHTHOUSE
(Equal 6 second interval of red light)

Established on Martha's Vineyard in 1828, this light station is located on the western side of the Edgartown inner harbor opposite Chappaquiddick Island.

The original light was in a tower on top of the keeper's house. It was replaced in 1939 by an 1875 cylindrical light tower which was floated by barge from Ipswich, Massachusetts. This was done in part to satisfy local residents who objected to the plans to replace the lighthouse station with a modern skeleton steel tower.

CAPE POGE LIGHTHOUSE
(White light flashing each 6 seconds)

Established on land purchased for thirty dollars in 1801, this lighthouse station began operating in 1802.

There have been at least three wooden towers at the site sitting on six or seven different locations being moved to accommodate the eroding coastal sand. The present tower matches plans of one to be built in 1893. This light is located on the Northeast point of Chappaquiddick Island which is off the tip of eastern Martha's Vineyard. It is one of the easternmost landfalls in New England and on the route to Edgartown Harbor. It is a flat, sandy spit of land with dunes and low scrub vegetation.

GAY HEAD LIGHTHOUSE

(Flashing white alternating with flashing red each 40 seconds)

The original lighthouse built on this site in 1799 was replaced with the present brick, brownstone, and steel tower built in 1856. It was fitted with a first order Fresnel lens which contained 1008 prisms. This lighthouse was considered one of the most important lights on the Atlantic coast and was one of the first in the country to be equipped with a Fresnel lens.

Gay Head Lighthouse is located on the westernmost point of land on the island of Martha's Vineyard. The light marks the Devil's Bridge rocks, the shoals of the south shore of the island, and the entrance to Vineyard Sound from Buzzard's Bay on the route to Boston Harbor from the South. The name Gay Head comes from the colorful clay bluffs below the area of the lighthouse.

The keeper's dwelling and other buildings have all been removed and only the automated and unmanned tower remains.

The Gay Head lighthouse site is surrounded by Wampanoag Tribal land. It is of interest to note that two of the most popular keepers of Gay Head Lighthouse were Gay Head Indians. Keeper Charles Wood Vanderhoop and his assistant Max Attaquin served from 1910 to 1933. Both had Gay Head Indian wives and raised families while serving at the station.

In the winter of 1884 the coast steamer "City of Columbus" hit the Devil's Bridge ledge which runs off shore from Gay Head below the lighthouse. Horace Pease, the lighthouse keeper at the time, led a crew of Indians in a daring rescue which saved many lives. Over 100 passengers drowned, however, within minutes of crashing into the ledge. Two of the men on the wreck were found to be frozen to death in the ships rigging and had to be cut loose from the icy ropes.

BRANT POINT LIGHTHOUSE

(Red light occulting for 4 seconds lighted 3 seconds)

Built in 1901, the present lighthouse tower is located at the end of the west side of the entrance to Nantucket Harbor. The long elevated wooden walkway across the sand to the lighthouse is a distinguishing feature of this small lighthouse. At only 26 feet tall it is the lowest lighthouse in New England.

This tower is the tenth lighthouse to be built in the vicinity of the light station. The first was built in 1746.

Two of the lighthouses burned down and at least two were destroyed by storms.

OLD BRANT POINT LIGHTHOUSE

This lighthouse built in 1856 is now a private residence and is part of the Coast Guard Station at Brant Point.

The former keeper's house is now the residence for the Officer in Charge.

SANKATY HEAD LIGHTHOUSE

(White light flashing each 7.5 seconds)

Built in 1849 and first lit in February of 1850, this lighthouse was so well built that the original tower still serves today. It is located on a cliff 60 feet above the water and is about one mile north of the town of Siaconset, Nantucket Island.

It's light, considered one of the brightest on the Atlantic, warns mariners of the Davis Southern Shoals. The light can be seen for up to 28 miles. The tower is unique in that it has a large red band in the center. The top and bottom portions are white.

GREAT POINT LIGHTHOUSE
(Flashing white with a red sector)

Originally established in 1784, this lighthouse located on the extreme northern tip of Nantucket Island was destroyed by a fire in 1816. It was replaced by a stone lighthouse tower which stood until a severe storm undermined it in 1985.

Construction was completed on a new stone lighthouse in the summer of 1986.

The many entries in a shipwreck log kept by the Great Point Lighthouse keepers bear out the fact that this is a very hazardous area for shipping.

Several wrecks were attributed in years past to Great Point's light being mistaken for the light from the lightship which was anchored at Cross Rip. A red sector was added to the light to warn of Cross Rip.

The importance of this lighthouse is seen by the fact that a Fresnel lens was installed in the Great Point Lighthouse in 1857.

HYANNIS HARBOR LIGHTHOUSE

This lighthouse in the harbor of Hyannis Port is a privately built lighthouse and is not an active lighthouse. It is located at the end of Channel Point Road. It can also be seen from the opposite side of the Harbor.

POINT GAMMON LIGHTHOUSE

This lighthouse built in 1816 is east of Hyannis Port. It is an inactive light and is now private property.

The light was discontinued in 1858 and the property was sold to private owners in 1872.

BASS RIVER LIGHTHOUSE

Completed in 1855, this lighthouse in West Dennis began operation April 30 of that year. The government discontinued the light August 1, 1880 and sold it at an auction. In 1881 it was repurchased by the government and reactivated until 1915 when the Cape Cod Canal was built. It became a private residence at that time. In the late 1930's it was purchased by the family of Senator Everett Stone. His family began accommodating summertime overnight guests and this developed into a guest home business which is now operated as "The Lighthouse Inn".

STAGE HARBOR LIGHTHOUSE

This west Chatham lighthouse built in 1880 was replaced by a white skeleton tower in 1933. The new light is a white light flashing every six seconds.

The old lighthouse is now a private dwelling. The lantern house has been removed from the tower.

CHATHAM LIGHTHOUSE STATION

(Group light flashing white twice each 10 seconds)

This light station established originally in 1808 consisted of twin wooden towers and a double keeper's dwelling. Samuel Nye, the first keeper, was appointed by President Thomas Jefferson. Sometime in the 1830's the wooden towers were replaced by brick ones which were first whitewashed and later painted white.

The southern tower of the two was rebuilt in 1863 and in 1877 the entire station was replaced across the street where it remains to this time.

The new towers were made of cast iron. In 1923 the north tower was removed to Nauset where it still serves.

The original lantern room of the current Chatham light is on display in the yard of the "Old Atwood House and Museum" in Chatham.

MONOMOY POINT LIGHTHOUSE

This lighthouse station established in 1823 was once the location of a fishing village which was founded in 1711. Now Monomoy Island is a barren strip of land extending from near Chatham ten miles to the south. The shifting sands have changed it from a peninsula to an island and back several times. The lighthouse now a half mile from shore was once situated near the dune line of the eastern shore.

Some time after 1923 when one of the twin lights at Chatham was removed, the Monomoy light was discontinued. The Cape Cod style keeper's house, the lighthouse tower, and a generator house, are all that reminds one of the former community that existed on this island. It is now a National Wilderness area. When operating, the lighthouse displayed a fixed white light with a red sector.

THE THREE SISTERS OF NAUSET LIGHTHOUSE STATION

This lighthouse station was established in 1838 on land purchased the previous year for $150 from the Collins family. The station was unique in that it had three brick lighthouse towers set in a row 150 feet apart on the bluff at Nauset.

Due to erosion of the bluffs the brick towers were replaced with three movable wooden towers in 1892.

These three lighthouses came to be known as "The Three Sisters of Nauset".

It was decided in 1911 that a revolving light with three flashes would be more effective than the three fixed lights. Two of the lights were discontinued and were sold to be used as beach cottages. The remaining single light came to be know as "The Beacon".

Remmants of the foundations of these lights reappear occasionally as they are uncovered by the tides washing the beach sands.

THE NAUSET BEACH LIGHTHOUSE

(Alternating red and white lights flashing each 5 seconds)

This lighthouse tower moved here from Chatham in 1923 is in the same general location as "The Three Sisters of Nauset" lighthouses.

The twin lights at Chatham also were changed to a single light in 1923. The north light which was discontinued was removed to Nauset Beach and replaced "The Beacon".

The wooden tower was sold to join the other two "Sisters of Nauset" as beach cottages. The tower moved to Nauset from Chatham was a cast iron tower and is the one now serving Nauset.

The three wooden towers known as "Three Sisters of Nauset" and also at other times "The Twin Lights" and "The Beacon" were purchased from their private owners by the National Park Service in 1975. Restoration of the towers and relocation to their original location near Coast Guard Beach is being considered by the National Park Service. The towers can presently be seen in a wooded area of the National Park Service property on the north side of Cable Road just a short distance from Nauset Beach Lighthouse.

HIGHLAND
LIGHTHOUSE STATION
(White light flashing each 5 seconds)

This lighthouse also called "Cape Cod Lighthouse" was first lit June 12, 1797.

It has always been considered a very important light as it marks the first landfall on the transatlantic route to Boston. The present brick lighthouse, keeper's house, and a generator shed, were built in 1857. A first order Fresnel lens was added at that time making it the most powerful light on the New England mainland. An additional keeper's house was added in 1961.

The lighthouse station is located on clay bluffs known as the "Truro Clay Pound". Several lighthouse towers stood on this site prior to the present one. It is surrounded by the National Park Service Cape Cod National Seashore. The light, 183 feet above the water can be seen 20 miles out to sea.

Many shipwrecks occurred in the area prior to the establishment of the light station. In 1794, the Reverend Levi Whitman wrote "that mountain of clay in Truro seems to have been erected in the midst of sand hills by the God of Nature for the foundation of a lighthouse, which, if it should be obtained, in time no doubt would save the lives of thousands".

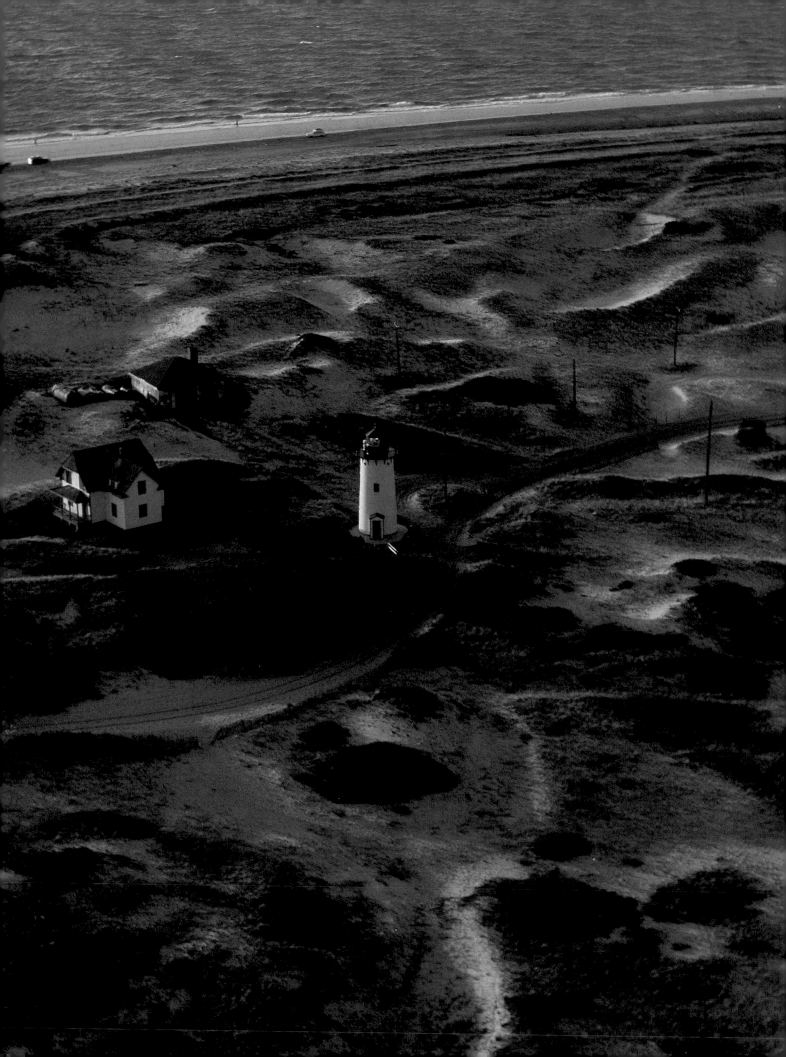

RACE POINT LIGHTHOUSE

(White light flashing each 15 seconds)

This lighthouse, established in 1816, marks the head of the Cape and has been the site of many shipwrecks.

Someone has estimated, that for every wreck that has occurred since the light was established, there were a dozen more that were saved by the light. Between 1816 and 1946 more than 100 shipwrecks were recorded at Race Point.

The present lighthouse and keeper's dwelling date back to 1876. This light station is the primary light guarding the entrance to the harbor of Provincetown. It is surrounded by sand dunes and is accessible only on foot or by four wheel drive. It is located within the Cape Cod National Seashore and access is restricted by the National Park Service.

There is some indication at present that the Coast Guard is developing plans to utilize and rehabilitate the complex in coordination with the National Park Service Cape Cod National Seashore.

WOOD END LIGHTHOUSE

(Red light flashing each 15 seconds)

First established as a white pyramidal navigational aid in 1864, followed by a wooden signal tower in 1872, the first and present lighthouse was built here in 1873. It is a square, white tower, a twin of the Long Point Lighthouse nearby. Wood End is located 1.5 miles due south across the harbor from Provincetown on the southerly coastline of the "arm" of Cape Cod that extends around the Provincetown Harbor.

LONG POINT LIGHTHOUSE

(Green flashing light)

This lighthouse station was first illuminated in 1827. It is located at the end of the "arm" of land which extends around Provincetown Harbor. It is approximately one mile east of Wood End Lighthouse and at the mouth of the harbor. This square white brick tower is identical to the one at Wood End.

SANDY NECK LIGHTHOUSE

Now privately owned and inactive, this former lighthouse was first established in 1827. The lighthouse was rebuilt in 1857 and is the one still standing.

The lighthouse is located at the western side of the entrance to Barnstable Harbor. The lantern room of this lighthouse has been removed.

Even though the lighthouse station is now the only remaining structure on the end of the sandy point, there was at one time a community of around two hundred people living there. A fishery, salt works, and several windmills which had shared the area were moved to Provincetown just before the Civil War. Two forts were built during that war and became known locally as "Fort Useless" and "Fort Harmless".

PLYMOUTH LIGHTHOUSE

(Group light flashing alternate single and double white every 20 seconds, includes a red sector)

This lighthouse station established by the Massachusetts Legislature in 1768, was ceded to the Federal Government in 1790. The original lighthouse building had a lantern at each end of the building thirty feet apart. This feature continued for 156 years until the northeast tower light was discontinued in 1924.

The lighthouse is situated on high bluffs at the point of the long peninsula which extends from Duxbury south to the entrance of Plymouth Harbor. This area is called "the Gurnet". It is thought that the name Gurnet came from islands by that name in the British Isles. They were named after a fish common in the area.

The Plymouth Lighthouse completely destroyed by fire in 1801 was again operational in 1803. It was rebuilt again in 1843. Temporary beacons were provided for the safety of mariners during these times.

During the Revolutionary War the towns of Plymouth, Duxbury, and Kingston joined in building a fort on the Gurnet. On the occasion of a battle with a British ship a cannonball pierced the lighthouse but did not affect the function of the light.

DUXBURY PIER LIGHTHOUSE

(Group light flashing red three times each 10 seconds)

This lighthouse known locally as "Bug Light" was built in Plymouth Harbor in 1871. It is a "spark plug" appearing lighthouse and is surrounded by water.

Lighthouse keeper Fred Bohm of Duxbury Pier Lighthouse became famous for his feats as a lifesaver. Ninety persons, including thirty-six girl scouts, were rescued by him in one year.

One woman was rescued from a capsized boat. She had become entangled in sea-weed and was unconscious when she was pulled on shore by the keeper who had to swim in after her.

Her first question on regaining consciousness was "Where are my clothes?". "I don't know, but you are lucky to be alive", Bohm reminded her.

SCITUATE LIGHTHOUSE

This lighthouse built in 1811 is now inactive and is owned by the town of Scituate. The keeper's house is the original 1811 house. The structure consists of the original 1811 stone lighthouse with its 1827 superstructure, 1847 modifications, and a 1930 lens room on top. The complex has been restored and is nicely maintained by the Scituate Historical Society.

The lighthouse was built on Cedar Point at the entrance of Scituate Harbor to accommodate the growing marine activity in the area at the time. The light at Scituate was discontinued November 14, 1860 with the lighting of the new Minot's Ledge Lighthouse which was illuminated the following day.

The first keeper of the Scituate Lighthouse was Simeon Bates. One of the most remarkable stories of the lighthouse involved his children during the War of 1812.

Alone at the lighthouse early one September day of 1814, the girls saw an approaching British warship. Rebecca and Abigal immediately sent their younger brother to warn the towns people of a possible onslaught from the big guns and warriors of the ship. They watched five landing boats start toward the shore near the lighthouse. They knew something had to be done.

Rebecca grabbed a drum belonging to a guardsman who should have been on duty and handed Abigal a fife. They began playing familiar martial tunes. They played louder and louder as the soldiers approached. The oarsmen stopped their rowing and listened.

The commander of the warship hearing the drum and fife feared the Americans were amassing to overcome them. He fired a warning shot to recall the landing party.

Another parting shot was fired at the lighthouse as they hastily left the harbor. The shot fell short of its mark and the girls and their "phantom army" had saved the day.

Needless to say, the keeper's children became instant celebrities for their courage and ingenuity which likely saved the town great loss of life and property.

MINOT'S LEDGE LIGHTHOUSE

(A group light flashing one, four, and three times each 45 seconds)

This lighthouse built on a twenty-five foot ledge in 1850 is considered one of the most dangerous locations in America. This ledge, just one mile offshore from Cohasset, is exposed only at lowest tide. This made the construction of the lighthouse one of the most hazardous ever attempted. Often the men working were washed into the sea by unexpected waves or surges. Twice during the construction of the first lighthouse tower the drilling equipment and working platform were swept away in summer storms.

The first lighthouse begun in 1847 was first lighted January 1, 1850. It was built on steel legs embedded in the rock.

The first keeper, Isaac Dunham, feeling the lighthouse structure was unsafe resigned in October after serving on the rock for only ten months. The new keeper at first belittled the safety issue until he had experienced a severe storm in the late fall of 1850. The new keeper then joined in requests that the lighthouse supports be strengthened.

A committee who examined it on a calm day decided against any improvement stating that it would withstand any storm.

Unfortunately, they were wrong and in a Spring storm of April 16, 1851 the lighthouse went down taking with it the two assistant lighthouse keepers. There was a consensus at the time that the storm presented the highest tide and wind force of any since the great storm of December, 1786.

The head keeper, John Bennett, due to the storm had been prevented from returning from Cohasset to the lighthouse. He was worried about his assistants. Restless, he walked along the beach during the night. Early the next morning he began to notice debris washing ashore from the storm. To his amazement he saw pieces of the lighthouse and even some of his own clothing. His fears about his assistants were confirmed when later the next day their bodies were found washed ashore.

The construction of the present stone lighthouse tower was one of great engineering, planning, and achievement. Begun in 1855, it was completed in 1860. The huge stones were cut to interlock with each surface with which they came in contact. Cement, steel shafts, and wooden pins were also used to make the construction secure. The first layer contained seven stones weighing over two tons each. The second course included twenty-nine stones. Each additional course was dovetailed in such a way that the pounding waves would lock them even tighter.

There was great celebrating when on August 22, 1860 the light was once again lit in Minot's Ledge Lighthouse. Lightships which were anchored nearby to provide a substitute for the missing tower light during this time of construction were no longer needed.

During 1987 and 1988, extensive repairs were made to the upper layers of the lighthouse. With the lantern room removed several layers of the top portion of the tower were replaced with new stones.

It is difficult to imagine these upper layers being damaged by the elements. When one takes in consideration the reports of giant waves actually going "over the top of the light" however, it becomes more understandable. The damaged stones we saw on shore during the repair project seemed to sustain damage primarily at the points where holes had been drilled for inserting the balcony metal rail supports.

Probably because of its danger and its tragic history, this light seems to have more superstition and lore attached to it than most other lights.

There are still rumors of the ghosts of the assistant keepers being heard and seen in the night amid severe storms.

Because of its signal, this light also has a romantic nature about it. The one, four, and three signal has caused it to be known as the "I Love You Light" or "Lovers Light".

There is an excellent museum in Cohasset sponsored by the Cohasset Historical Society which contains many artifacts, pictures, and other information about the Minot's Ledge Lighthouse. We would highly recommend that you visit the museum and share the nostalgia of this historic lighthouse.

BOSTON LIGHT
(White light flashing each 10 seconds)

This lighthouse built in Boston Harbor on Little Brewster Island in 1716 has the distinction of being the first lighthouse built in America. It was built as a result of petitions by the local merchants to the General Court of Massachusetts in 1713. The court concurred and by September 4, 1716 the lighthouse was illuminated for the first time.

There were earlier mentions of beacons in Boston Harbor but these were not thought to be what we know as lighthouses but rather a tower or pole with a fire or lantern on it as a marker. In 1679, a Dutchman, Jasper Danker, wrote in his diary of a beacon on Little Brewster Island.

A cannon at the Boston Light became the America's first fog signal in 1718. A more conventional fog signal was added in 1890.

A fire burned all of the wooden parts of the lighthouse in 1751. Later in 1775 American troops intentionally set fire to the lighthouse to keep it from being of use to the British. The tower being largely of stone was soon under repair by the British under protection of marine guard.

Troops dispatched by General George Washington defeated the guard and destroyed their repairs. A year later when the British fleet left Boston one of their last acts was to blow up the lighthouse tower. The Governor of Massachusetts, John Hancock, appeared before the Legislature in 1780 to promote the rebuilding of the light. This was done in the early 1780's.

A good way to see this and other lighthouses in Boston Harbor is to take one of the several boat cruises to the islands of the outer harbor. From George's Island a free water taxi is available in the summertime to transport passengers to other islands such as Little Brewster.

The Boston Lighthouse is one of the last lights in the country to be manned by Coast Guard keepers. Being of such great value as a navigational aid and also as a valuable historic treasure it will likely continue to have favorable consideration by the Coast Guard to be a manned and active lighthouse station.

LONG ISLAND HEAD LIGHTHOUSE
(Flashing white light)

Boston Harbor's second lighthouse was built on Long Island in the inner harbor in 1819. It was known as "The Inner Harbor Light" for many years. It has been situated in at least three places on the end of Long Island since it was first established.

A signal system was devised at this light to indicate when there was a need for additional harbor pilots. A black ball was hoisted when there was a need for a pilot.

NIX'S MATE DAYMARK

This non-lighthouse navigational aid is an example of an aid called a "daymark". Located along the main route into Boston Harbor, it was once a popular place for hanging and displaying captured pirates.

DEER ISLAND
(Alternating red and white light flashing each 10 seconds with a red sector)

The Deer Island lighthouse which was built in 1890 no longer exists. It was razed and replaced by a "matchstick" type modular light just off shore from the east end of Deer Island.

47

THE GRAVES LIGHTHOUSE

(White light flashing twice each 12 seconds)

The Graves Lighthouse is one of the newer lighthouses in Massachusetts. Under construction for two years it was completed in the summer of 1905. Seen by many on the approach to Logan International Airport, this stately granite tower has the appearance of a much older lighthouse.

The Graves Ledge might have been named because of its reputation as the site of many shipping tragedies. It was in actuality named for Vice Admiral Thomas Graves of John Winthrop's fleet. Winthrop was a well known resident of nearby Lynn, Massachusetts.

Sitting on solid rock just four feet above the low tide water level, the tower serves also as the keeper's house. The first level is a giant stone cistern thirty-five feet in height and thirty feet in diameter at the base on the outside. While keepers were living in the lighthouse before automation, the cistern was filled twice yearly with fresh water brought by a lighthouse tender.

The second stage of the lighthouse above the water supply is an engine room for the diesel engines which were installed to operate a fog horn. The third level was the kitchen and the fourth the sleeping quarters. A fifth level served as a living area and included a library and watch room. The next three levels up contained the light machinery and the light itself.

The Graves Lighthouse was fitted with a first order Fresnel lens from Paris and was for many years the most powerful light in New England.

MARBLEHEAD LIGHTHOUSE

(Fixed green light)

This lighthouse station was first established on the north point of Marblehead Neck on the east side of the entrance to Marblehead Harbor in 1833 by the town of Marblehead. The first tower, later obscured by new development, was replaced as the light source by a 100 foot mast with a light mounted on it. The present 105 foot cast iron and steel tower was built in 1895 by the United States Lighthouse Service.

This unique tower consists of a cast iron pipe-like center shaft supported with a system of steel braces. The center shaft contains a spiral staircase of 105 steps to a platform on which rests the lamp room and lens room. There are outside balconies on both the lamp room and lens room levels.

FORT PICKERING LIGHTHOUSE
(Flashing white light)

This lighthouse is located between Beverly and Salem at the Winter Island Park recreational area on the site of old Fort Pickering. This small lighthouse was built in 1871. Only the tower still remains of this light station. It is quite well preserved as a part of the recreational area at the site of what was also once a seaplane base. Its light still serves to guide water traffic into Salem Harbor. Baker's Island and Derby Wharf Lighthouses can both be easily seen from this light.

The Fort Pickering Lighthouse once had a keeper who was removed for not being on the job. He hired a proxy keeper while he took a job as a superintendent of a nearby reform school. His lighthouse service superindentent felt he should reform and relieved him of this lighthouse duties.

DERBY WHARF LIGHTHOUSE
(Flashing red light each 6 seconds)

Derby Wharf is located in the Maritime National Historic Site, Salem.

This 12 foot square lighthouse built in 1870, sits on the very end of Derby Wharf. The name came from two well known Salem merchants, Richard and Elias Derby, who paid for the construction of 803 feet of the structure between 1764 and 1771. Another 1300 feet was added between 1806 and 1808.

Being close to Salem it was never necessary for this lighthouse to have a resident keeper. The Coast Guard decommissioned the light in 1977 and in 1979 it was turned over to the National Park Service.

An organization called The Friends of Salem Maritime, organized in 1983, worked with the Park Service to restore the Derby Wharf lighthouse. There is also a lighthouse exhibit sponsored by these two organizations with the Coast Guard and the Peabody Museum of Salem.

HOSPITAL POINT LIGHTHOUSE

(12,000 candlepower fixed light)

This lighthouse built in 1872 is officially listed by the Coast Guard as "Hospital Point Range Front Light".

It forms a range light with a powerful light in the steeple of the Beverly First Baptist Church to guide ships into the main channel of Salem Harbor, It is located at the end of Bayview Avenue in Beverly.

The strategic value of this point was recognized as early as 1711 when a watch station was established on the site. A fort was added in 1775.

The name comes from the hospital for smallpox victims which was located on the Point in 1801. The

hospital became a military barracks during the War of 1812. In 1849 the hospital was completely destroyed by fire.

In 1871 a temporary lighthouse was established and the permanent facility now in use was constructed a year later. The light became a range light with the Baptist Church steeple in 1927.

Hospital Point Lighthouse became an unmanned, automated light in 1947. The keeper's home was designated as private living quarters for the Commander of the First Coast Guard District. He is responsible for Coast Guard activities in Massachusetts, Maine, New Hampshire, Rhode Island, and most of Vermont. The First District headquarters is in Boston.

HOSPITAL POINT
REAR RANGE LIGHT

This 28,000 candlepower fixed light located in the steeple of the Beverly First Baptist Church forms a range light with the light at Hospital Point Lighthouse to guide vessels along the main ship channel into Salem. It seems appropriate to me that a church should be a point of light and guidance! Hopefully, the majority are in many ways.

* Note: My travels to photograph and gather information about this book took me all over the state of Massachusetts. I would like to commend the town of Beverly as a considerate, courteous, and helpful community. Even the drivers seemed to take more care for pedestrians.

Thanks goes to the Fist Baptist Church also for letting me get a good look at their light in the steeple.

BAKER'S ISLAND LIGHTHOUSE

(Alternating white and red light flashing each 20 seconds)

Baker's Island Lighthouse marks the outer harbor of the once very busy port of Salem. The station was first established in 1798 after having been authorized by Congress in 1796.

The keeper's house is now a private residence.

The original keeper's house was attached between two lighthouse towers. In 1817 one of the lights was discontinued. Due to several tragic shipwrecks which were blamed on the confusion caused by not having two lights which identified the station as expected, the government restored the second light in 1820. It was again discontinued when the government determined single lights with unique signals were better. The present higher lighthouse tower was built in 1821 and a new brighter beacon was installed in 1916.

EASTERN POINT LIGHTHOUSE
(White light flashing each 5 seconds)

The land for this lighthouse station and a two mile access right of way around the cove was purchased from S.G. Burnam in 1829 for $300. Construction was completed and this lighthouse showing the way to Gloucester Harbor became functional in 1832. Unmanned and automated in 1986, the station still serves as housing for Coast Guard personnel with other duties.

A very scenic area, this station was the home to the American artist Homer Winslow during the year of 1880. His work done while living at the lighthouse is some of his most famous.

The Massachusetts Historical Commission indicates that Eastern Point Lighthouse Station is the state's largest intact station dating back to the late nineteenth century.

GLOUCESTER BREAKWATER LIGHT
(Red light occulting every 4 seconds)

This light is actually part of the Eastern Point Lighthouse station and was maintained by the same keepers. It is built at the end of a long breakwater built out from Eastern Point over Dog Bar Reef. In stormy and freezing weather this breakwater path to the lighthouse was very hazardous for the keeper. Now automated, this is not so much a problem. This beacon type light is mounted on a steel skeleton tower. A small building still part of the tower served for storage and shelter.

TEN POUND ISLAND LIGHTHOUSE
(Equal interval red light each 6 seconds)

This lighthouse built in 1821 is the most easily seen of the lighthouses in the Gloucester area. Ten Pound Island is located within the harbor.

Amos Story, a keeper of this lighthouse, in a sworn statement told of seeing a "sea serpent" from a distance of no more than twenty rods. He told of seeing at least 50

feet of the monster and described how the animal carried his head up out of the water.

Ten Pound Island Lighthouse was recently awarded a federal grant of $17,000 for restoration. The amount will be matched by the City of Gloucester. It is hoped that eventually the Coast Guard will allow the relighting of Ten Pound Island Light as a private navigational aid.

THATCHER'S ISLAND TWIN LIGHTHOUSES
(White light flashing five times at 20 second intervals)

This twin light station, also known as "Cape Ann Lighthouse", was established in 1771. Its first keeper a Captain Kirkwood, was removed as keeper during the Revolutionary war by the Minute Men due to his being a Tory. The lights remained unlighted during the war.

The first two towers were 45 feet in height but were replaced by 124 foot towers equipped with first order Fresnel lenses in 1861. Originally, it was thought that double lights could be more easily identified. Eventually, this idea was discounted and all multiple lights were reduced to single lights. The north light on Thatcher's Island was discontinued in 1932.

The twin lights on Thatcher's Island are the only ones of the eight multiple lights on the Atlantic coast which remain intact.

A tragedy was averted in 1919 when the S.S. America carrying President Woodrow Wilson and his staff were returning from Europe. The ship was on a collision course with Thatcher's Island, blinded by a dense fog. The faithful sounding of the fog signal was heard and the course was changed in time to save the ship and its passengers.

Another story is told of this light regarding a storm arising while the keeper Bray was away due to taking a sick assistant to Rockport for treatment. A severe snowstorm came up and the two lights had to be cared for every five hours by the wife who also had two small children to care for. Snowdrifts, darkness, and high wind made the task exhausting but the keeper's wife realized that lives, including that of her husband, may be at stake. She faithfully struggled back and forth to the lights to keep them burning.

When the keeper finally arrived back after correcting his course on sighting the familiar twin lights, the family spent a happy Christmas Day grateful that their lives had been spared and they were once again together.

In 1975 the Rockport Town Selectmen appointed a committee to give attention to the interests of maintenance and preservation of the lighthouses on Thatcher Island. The Thatcher Island Association was formed as a non-profit organization to provide a broader base of support for these purposes. This organization is working with the Coast Guard and the National Fish and Wildlife Commission to restore the North Light. Federal funds have been made available to make some of the recent improvements possible.

Two families serve as volunteer lighthouse keeper's to help maintain and protect the lights. Armand and Betty Desharnais who serve in the winter and George and Dottie Carrol who serve in the summer have been greatly appreciated for the work they have done to maintain the premises and to make it a pleasant place to visit.

The name of the island comes from the fact that the island was purchased from the heirs of Anthony Thatcher (often spelled Thacher). He was given the island by the General Court of Massachusetts after he and his wife were the only survivors in a shipwreck there in the 1635 hurricane.

STRAITSMOUTH ISLAND LIGHTHOUSE
(Green light flashing every 6 seconds)

This lighthouse was built in 1835 on Straitsmouth Island. The island is a short distance southeast from Rockport. Land for the lighthouse was purchased by the Federal Government from Aaron and Solomon Poole for $600 in 1834. The entire island, with the exception of the land the lighthouse tower is on, is now owned by the Massachusetts Audubon Society as a bird and wildlife sanctuary.

The Coast Guard owns and maintains the tower. A keeper's house, oilhouse, and two other out buildings still remain in addition to the lighthouse tower.

The lighthouse was converted to solar power in 1985.

ANNISQUAM HARBOR LIGHTHOUSE

(White light flashing every 7.5 seconds with red sector)

This attractive lighthouse built on Wigwam Point at the mouth of the Annisquam River was first established in 1801. The original wooden tower was replaced by the existing brick tower in 1897. The keeper's house is now used as a residence for Coast Guard personnel.

Being a little difficult to find by road, it is most seen by those traveling by boat.

If in Rockport the way to the light is to follow Route 127 to Annisquam Village Church and turn right. There will be a small "Annisquam" sign and also an indication that this is Leonard Street. Turn right into Norwood Heights and follow the circular road around to the lighthouse. It is well worth the trouble for the visit.

The friendly village of Annisquam is just beyond Norwood Heights on Leonard Street. The Annisquam Exchange offers crafts and other collectibles for sale. A historical society museum in the village is also worthy of a visit.

NEWBURYPORT HARBOR LIGHTHOUSE

(Group occulting green light flashing each 15 seconds)

This lighthouse station originally established in 1788 is located on the north end of Plum Island at the mouth of the Merrimack River. The present tower was built in 1898. The original station included two small lighthouse towers.

Due to the shifting sands in the channel these first lights were moved several times. Jetties were built to stop the channel from shifting and when this stabilized the shoreline the present more permanent light was built.

There is some indication that its construction incorporated some elements of one of the original twin lights. If it is one of the original twin lights it would be the oldest light still standing in the state.

In 1981 the fourth order Fresnel lens in the lighthouse was replaced by a fully automatic plastic lens. This lighthouse tower also includes a microwave radar and closed circuit automated television camera which enables the Merrimack River Coast Guard Station in Newburyport to monitor the activity in the channel.

NEWBURYPORT FRONT RANGE TOWER

The Front Range Tower, built in 1873 on Bayley's Wharf, was moved to its present location at the Coast Guard Station in the 1960's. It is no longer an active light but serves as a daymark. In the original location this range light and The Rear Range Tower were very helpful in guiding mariners into the channel.

NEWBURYPORT REAR RANGE TOWER

This tower also, built in 1873, is located on Water Street and is now a private residence. The range lights were discontinued in 1961. These range lights as well as the tower of the lighthouse on Plum Island are included in the National Registry of Historic Places.

Little Lighthouse

Who are you, you little spark
Poking holes in the starless dark,
Intermittent flash of light,
Piercing fog-filled stormy night?
Where you stand is on the way
Where shoal and sandbar dangers lay,
Where ragged rocks do wreck and
plunder,
Smashing ships and boats asunder.
Your message from the lantern room
Transcends the black and deadly gloom,
Warns mariners to turn their wheel,
Outwit the great bell's death knell peal.
Little lighthouse there you stand
On stony bluff above the sand,
Mid sea gulls cry and hurricane
Sun and snow and freezing rain.
Your past is strewn with courage,
bravery is your guest
Your faithfulness to duty
never took a rest.
Mystical, romantic,
your time is done.
Automated towers,
their age has just begun.
So you slip into the past,
as everyone must go,
But you've made your place in space,
a spot on hero's row.
When my time has come
to follow nature's plan,
May they say of me, like you,
that I served my fellow man.

Poem by Betty Scott

LIGHTSHIPS

Lightships served as floating lighthouses anchored near dangerous waters where building a lighthouse was impractical or impossible. Coast Guardsmen who served on these floating beacons stayed at their posts through fog, storms, and even hurricanes. In modern times, automated light towers and huge buoys have replaced the ships.

There are four lightships which have served in Massachusetts waters or which can still be seen now in Massachusetts at the present time.

NEW BEDFORD LIGHTSHIP

This lightship which is now on display by the Coast Guard in New Bedford was built in 1930. It was designated as #114 (WAL536). It served as The Lightship Portland and was renamed New Bedford after being decommissioned.

NANTUCKET LIGHTSHIP
#112 (WAL534)

This lightship built in 1936 was one of several which served on the Nantucket Shoals. It is now privately owned and has been on display in Nantucket as a museum. It appears that it no longer will be on display in Nantucket but will be berthed at a pier in the harbor of Portland, Maine. This ship was originally paid for by the British as compensation for one which was cut in half in a collision by the British ship "Olympic".

Hurricane Edna pounded this ship with 110 mile per hour winds and waves 70 feet high in 1954.

The Nantucket served in Portland, Maine during World War II. It was fitted with deck guns and was assigned to be a harbor entrance control vessel. It is now owned by a preservation group, Nantucket Lightship Preservation, Inc. It is their plan to have it on display in Portland as a lightship museum.

NANTUCKET I LIGHTSHIP
(WLV612)

This lightship, built in 1950, is also now privately owned and is berthed in Boston at the docks in Charlestown near the ship "The Constitution".

It was used as a drug interdiction vessel off the coast of Florida after its service as a lightship near Nantucket ended. It was found impractical for this purpose and sold to private owners interested in preserving it.

NANTUCKET II LIGHTSHIP
(WLV613)

This lightship, built in 1952, was the last one to serve on the Nantucket Shoals. It served in many other areas as well as a relief ship. Built in 1952, this ship was decommissioned in 1984. It is now jointly sponsored as a lightship exhibit by the New England Seaport and the Lighthouse Preservation Society. It is owned by the New England Seaport Trust.

NEW HAMPSHIRE LIGHTHOUSES

ISLES OF SHOALS LIGHTHOUSE
(White light flashing each 15 seconds)

The first Isles of Shoals Lighthouse was built on White Island in 1820. It was rebuilt to be a granite tower in 1885 during the Civil War. One famous keeper of this lighthouse was Thomas B. Leighton. He was also owner of four of the islands in The Isles of Shoals. His daughter, Cecila, became even more known for her poem, "The Sandpiper", which is partially included below.

Across the narrow beach we flit
  One little sandpiper and I,
And fast I gather bit by bit,
  The scattered driftwood, bleached and
dry.

The wild waves reach their hands for it,
  The wild winds raves, the tide runs
high,

As up and down the beach we flit
  The little sandpiper and I.
Above our heads the sullen clouds
  Scud black and swift across the sky;
Like silent ghosts in misty shrouds
  Stand out the white lighthouses high.
Comrade, where wilt thou be to-night
  When the loosened storm breaks
furiously?

My driftwood fire will burn so bright!
  To what warm shelter canst thou fly?
I do not fear for thee, though wroth
  The tempest rushes through the sky:
For are we not God's children both —
  Thou, little sandpiper, and I?

WHALEBACK LIGHT
(White light flashing twice each ten seconds)

This lighthouse, built in 1820, has born the brunt of many severe storms. The original tower, badly damaged by heavy seas, was replaced by a new tower completed in 1872.

Although this light is often listed as being in New Hampshire (since it protects the Portsmouth harbor), it is actually closer to the Maine coast. It is best seen from Fort Foster which is reached from Kittery, Maine.

FORT POINT LIGHTHOUSE
(Fixed green light)

This lighthouse, first established in 1771, marks the inner harbor of Portsmouth. It is located in the historic town of New Castle. The lighthouse is part of a large U.S. Coast Guard station and on the site of old Fort Constitution which was called Fort William and Mary before the Revolutionary War.

The tower is 88 feet in height and the station includes a fog signal which gives a blast each 10 seconds.

Epilogue

A friend of ours wrote the foregoing poem after visiting a lighthouse on the West coast. Lighthouses seem to inspire talent. Longfellow was moved to write as he often visited the Portland Head Lighthouse in Maine. American artist Homer Winslow is credited with creating some of his best works of art during the year he lived at Eastern Point Lighthouse in Gloucester.

Even politicians seem to agree when it comes to supporting efforts and expense to maintain and preserve our nation's historic lights. Something about lighthouses seems to lift our spirits and our pride in the history of our country's growth and development.

Technology has changed the significance and function of the lighthouse but it hasn't changed our sense of caring for our fellow man and the safeguards we provide for his safety on the water.

Even though automated, the lights still shine in most places. Where they have been extinguished there generally is something better.

Lighted buoys, modular towers or perhaps a new lighthouse with a more powerful light or more easily distinguished signal, has replaced them.

Radio communications, radar, Loran navigational equipment, and more powerful electronic fog signals have all contributed to improved navigational safety.

The modern Coast Guard cutter and the Coast Guard helicopter, called to action by ship to shore radio, have made lifesaving more effective than ever.

The lighthouse still has a function even though its light may not be as indispensable as in the past. It seems to me that this institution of the past is serving more than just to send its light over the water.

It seems to me that the lighthouse notably serves to remind us of our heritage of courage and self-sacrifice in behalf of others. It is a monument to the courageous men and women who often braved the darkness, the freezing cold, and the violent storm, to save their fellow man.

The lives of many are still in jeopardy in the storms of life. It may be in illness, homelessness, poverty, or the tides of misfortune or tragedy.

Hopefully, the lighthouse, a symbol of our caring heritage, will remind us to throw a lifeline to those in need.

If these are valid reflections, it seems important that we maintain and preserve these historic treasures!

BIBLIOGRAPHY AND SOURCES

Holland, Francis Ross,
America's Lighthouse,
Stephen Green Press, Brattleboro,
VT 1972.

Snow, Edward Rowe,
The Lighthouses of New England,
Dodd, Mead & Company, New
York, NY 1973.

"Lighthouses and Other Aids to the
Mariner",
Newport News, VA., 1946.

Lighthouses and Lightships of the
U.S.,
Boston, Houghton-Mifflin, 1917.
Smith, Arthur,

Lighthouses,
Houghton-Mifflin, 1971.
Stockridge, Truman R.,

Chronology of Aids to Navigation
and the Old Lighthouse Service:
1716-1939,
1939.Adams, William H.D.,

Lighthouses and Lightships, N.Y. and
London,
Nelson and Sons, 1871.
Beaver, Patrick,

A History of Lighthouses,
Citadel Press, 1976.
Collins, F.A.,

Sentinels Along the Coast,
New York, The Century Co., 1922.
Hague, D.L.,

Lighthouses, Architecture, and
History and Archaeology.

Famous Lighthouses of New England,
Boston, Yankee Public, Co., 1945.

Thompson, Frederick L.,
The lightships of Cape Cod,
Congress Square Press, Portland,
ME, 1983.

Thanks to these public officials who
are working to preserve the wealth of
historic treasure found in the State of
Massachusetts and especially for their
efforts in behalf of preserving the
lighthouses of Massachusetts. The
nomination and acceptance of the
majority of the lighthouses of
Massachusetts to the National
Registry of Historical Places was
accomplished largely by the hard
work and influence of these
individuals. Their research for this
purpose has been of great help to me
in gathering information for this
book.

Michael Joseph Connolly, Secretary
of State.
Valerie A. Talmage, Executive
Director of the Massachusetts
Historical Comm., and State
Historic Preservation Officer.
Anne Tait, Survey Coordinator,
Massachusetts Historical
Commission.
Betsy Friedburg, National Registry of
Historical Places/Director.

Poem, "Keeper of the Light" from fall
1985 Keeper's Log U.S. Lighthouse
Society - Used by Permission

My appreciation also to Mr. Ray
Empey, lighthouse hobbyist and
authority, for sharing his vast
knowledge of the Massachusetts
lighthouses.

Pam Steiner, my secretary, was a
great help with the word processor.

My wife, Jo, was both helpful and
encouraging as we gathered
information and photographs
together.

Special thanks to pilot Merrill C.
Patten Jr. who enabled us to get our
aerial photographs, and got us safely
to our destination.

Others which I would recommend to
you as resources for lighthouse
information and materials are:

MR. KEN BLACK, DIRECTOR
Shore Village Museum
104 Limerock St.
Rockland, ME 04841
An excellent museum primarily of
lighthouse artifacts and materials.

MR. WAYNE WHEELER
United States Lighthouse Society
244 Kearny St., 5th Floor
San Francisco, CA 94108
An outstanding non-profit historical
and educational society whose
membership includes several
thousand lighthouse enthusiasts.
Publication, The Keepers Log is filled
with lighthouse information.

MASSACHUSETTS CHAPTER
United States Lighthouse Society
314 Spring Street
Hanson, MA 02341

FRIENDS OF THE BOSTON
HARBOR ISLANDS
P.O. Box 9025
Boston, MA 02114

······~······

Library of Congress Cataloging in
Publication data:

AUTHOR:
Wally Welch

PUBLISHER:
Lighthouse Publications

Library of Congress
Catalog Number: 89-83935
ISBN 0-9618410-2-8

Color separations and printing done
in Hong Kong by Everbest Printing
Co., Ltd. through Four Color
Imports, Ltd., Louisville, KY.

DESIGNER:
Derek Dugan